Dipper
in danger

Written by Monica Hughes

Illustrated by Robert McPhillips

Heinemann

Dipper was a dolphin.
She was happy in the sea.
One day Dipper swam off to find
some fish to eat.

Dipper swam down and down.
She saw a fish.
'I will eat that fish,' she said.

Dipper swam down, down, down.
She saw a squid.
'I will eat that squid,' she said.

Just then Dipper saw a net.
The net went over Dipper.

Dipper tried to get out of the net.
She tried to go up.

She tried to go down.
But she could not get out of the net.

Dipper was sad.

'What can I do?' she said.

'I can't get out.'

Then Dipper looked up
and saw a diver.
The diver saw Dipper in the net.

The diver went up to Dipper.
She made a hole in the net
so that Dipper could get out.

Dipper tried to get out of the net
but the hole was too little.

So the diver made a big hole
so that Dipper could get out
of the net.

Dipper was very happy.
So was the diver.
They swam off over the sea.